An Epistle on Mercy

Other Titles in the Series
Letters to the Devoted Follower of Christ

(in the order in which they were written)

An Epistle to the Miserable
An Epistle to the Moderately Miserable
An Epistle on Judgment
An Epistle on the Tripartite Nature of Man
An Epistle on Mercy

AN EPISTLE
ON MERCY

By

A Little Anchor of the Church

An Epistle

on Mercy

Greetings to you, my valued friend in Christ. I earnestly pray my words contain only truth and that they help you comprehend God better. May the Holy Spirit enlighten you where my words have been insufficient to convey the great meaning God's Truth holds in all Its manifest forms. As I have stated before, any errors are mine, and all truths are revealed by

God. All glory and honor rightly belong to Him.

It seemed natural to turn to the subject of God's mercy after speaking of His judgment.

God's heart must grieve at how easily His people interpret His mercy as intent to place upon them difficult trials. He is never the originator of the trials in our lives, in His Church, or in our nations. Sin and evil are — the forces of the world, the flesh, and the devil. God has simply covenanted Himself to respect the freedom to choose with which Man was endowed. And for this liberality He is continually judged as harsh because we have erroneously concluded that since He has the power to halt all evil, He wrongs us when He does not.

Many Christians seem to get the theory of God and His ways quite well, but when the enemy sends a crisis, or sends others to them with questions when some crisis brings them freshly to mind (having taken little thought of them between these trials), their practical applications often do not come into solid agreement with their theory. It is like this regarding the subject of God's mercy. And really, we all need to continue to learn more about God and His ways. No matter how much we know, there is always more to learn.

FOLLOWERS of Christ are expected to exercise their faith, and faith is especially needful during times of crisis when trying to comprehend matters of judgment and mercy. We nurture faith in the everyday so that when the special days come, its stores of trust and Christ-virtues will be at hand for us to rely on during seasons of pressing through disasters that happen around us. For some reason we tend to conclude that disasters happening around us mean they ought to have happened to us, or that God must have been negligent in our care for them to hit so close to home, and our faith is tested regarding His goodness. Or we are just plain resentful when they strike a direct hit at us.

It is through our faith that we reconcile as best we can why a disaster hit us, someone else and not us, or why we had to partake in it to some extent, such as when we survive but some of those near us pass on ahead to that greater Land. Where was

God's mercy? What did it look like? If we do not reconcile these questions, they eat away at the soul. And God's heart yearns for us to be able to reconcile them somehow.

It is written that all true believers have been gifted with some measure of faith: "For I say, through the grace given unto me, to every man that is among you, not to think of himself more highly than he ought to think; but to think soberly, according as God hath dealt to every man the measure of faith."[*] Just as we are not to think of our self as more than we are (e.g., we are not gods), the principle also holds true that we ought not write off our responsibility to exercise our faith by declaring God gave us none. Neither ought we think of our self as less than God wants us to. Both invite problems. Every believer has a measure of faith, just as every believer has an identity in Christ, and both ought to be reaffirmed.

Since to become a believer at all requires a measure of faith, there is no valid reason why we do not continue to possess all the rest of our days at least this measure of faith

---

[*] Romans 12:3

in the God who saved our soul for eternal life, especially when we continue to count on it for upon-death salvation. Yet some seem to utilize their faith for this alone. No wonder they cannot open their eyes to what God is accomplishing in this earth in these days, for they have not the faith to see them through these many crises—they do not know what to hold onto while God is shaking everything that can be shaken.* So it became easier simply to deny that any

---

* Hebrews 12:26-27; and see Haggai 2:6-9. Please note well that it is God's purview to shake an individual's life at any time. Shaking to dislodge what is not anchored in Him is the spiritual principle to which He has committed Himself (Heb. 12:25—that He would dwell among the people was His covenant to them, and He did not defeat a pantheon of gods so they could break forth in order to continue to follow evil ways). God will not just release spirits *He* created into eternal death without doing everything possible to awaken them to the truth of their choice, or the truth of lifestyle choices that are wrecking their lives and robbing them of any reward they might have when they do get to Heaven by the skin of their teeth. We do not earn citizenship in Heaven by our good behavior; but how we live can gradually sear our conscience toward things God looks upon as evil, and then we become testimonies for those lifestyles instead of for God. Shaking the earth in a corporate manner in preparation for the end-of-days era is simply an application of this principle, albeit one of its greatest, widespread applications.

special shaking is occurring. We have to have eyes to see that Christ-Rock which travels with us,* to which we can anchor ourselves so that God's shaking will not displace us. God's Word promises us that His "mercy endureth for ever."† So we exercise our measure of faith in His Word so that we will not be shaken from that Rock.

Regardless how things look on every side, I believe God is laboring night and day to ensure that we receive His mercy at all times because He made a Blood Covenant with us. His Son's *Blood* pleads for us.

Part of what it means to be in blood covenant with another is making a commitment to come to your ally's aid when he is attacked, when disaster has struck, or if one

---

* I Corinthians 10:4

† II Chronicles 20:21-22—"And when he had consulted with the people, he appointed singers unto the LORD, and that should praise the beauty of holiness, as they went out before the army, and to say, Praise the LORD; for His mercy endureth for ever. And when they began to sing and to praise, the LORD set ambushments against the children of Ammon, Moab, and mount Seir, which were come against Judah; and they were smitten." See also Psalm 136:1, 2, 3, etc., where "His mercy endureth forever" is repeated in every verse in this psalm.

is in need and the other has a way to allevi-
ate that need. If we wonder whether God
will mercifully come to our aid in rescuing
us from this present darkness,* then we are
wondering whether He is going to uphold
the terms of His side of the Blood Covenant
He made with us—and I capitalize it because it is the highest form of this covenant
that can be made. Is God's arm so short to
save that the only way He can show mercy
to His Church is to catch them away? Is
there no other way at all His mercy can
manifest itself for us and for those still
awaiting salvation? And, oh, did I mention
it is a *BLOOD* Covenant?

God had the power to strike down in an
instant those who laid a hand on His Son.
Instead He spared Him not but delivered
Him into enemy hands so that His Blood
could be spilled for the remission of our
sins. Jesus did not just exchange a few
drops of blood with us, as is done when
sealing such a covenant. God permitted His
Son's Blood to be *liberally poured out* to
ensure the salvation of all humanity. So

---

* Ephesians 6:12

"how shall He not with Him also freely give us all things?"*

It is grievous that not all will receive this all-sufficient act of atonement wrought for them by the unrecognizable form of One who was pierced for *our* transgressions, not His; but for God's part, He did not stint. Jesus told His followers (of whom we are some), "This cup is the new testament in My blood, *which is shed for you.*"† Expressing to God that we do not expect Him to remember the Covenant of mercy He made with us is like telling Him not to remember the Blood that spilled out of His Son's body when He cruelly suffered in going to the Cross. We are in Blood Covenant with God, and He never forgets this. So take comfort that there is on the other side of this Cove-

---

* Romans 8:32

† Luke 22:20, emphasis added. By declaring this to be true the evening before His execution, we have the assurance that Jesus endured the Cross by His own will to do so. That is, He knew His Blood would need to be shed for us, and He did nothing to hinder the course of events. He could have chosen to leave the city that night, but instead we have the comfort of being able to trust in our Lord who did not fail to do what was necessary for our salvation. In like manner, can we not trust Him for all other things?

nant One who will keep its terms better than we can.

We must pray through eyes of faith to determine how God's mercy is working itself out in the crises of these days. Many times events have nothing to do with God's judgment but are vicious attacks from an enemy who not only seeks to steal and destroy some part of our life, but also to *kill*. "The thief cometh not, but for to steal, and to kill, and to destroy." We tend to get hung up on the bad news and forget the good news. And very often by our words and by the negligence of exercising our faith, we nullify the good news by receiving into our soul the bad news. Does not John 10:10 also declare, by Jesus Himself, "I am come that they might have life, and that they might have it more abundantly"?

The enemy mimics acts of judgment as a means of us maligning God's character of our own free will.* Yet God's mercy comes

---

* For the doing of our will carries more power of darkness because certain things are extremely difficult to accomplish in this earth as they have been appointed to be done through Man; so whichever side—light or dark—can successfully garner Man's help, this aids that side tremendously.

to our aid whether those acts are from His hand or the enemy's.

Jesus is always the counter to the evils of this world. He is God's mercy to us so that we will be saved alive for the glory of His Kingdom — though do not conclude that those who pass into Heaven before us were not saved alive. They were saved alive for all time and forever by being taken out of enemy reach. They live in the Kingdom's central hub, we at its adjunct locations; and we all are about the Kingdom business; we are all servants of the Father's household. We grieve for our own losses and for those they left behind, but do not say God failed to save them alive, for this is blatantly untrue. "And it shall come to pass, that whosoever shall call on the name of the Lord shall be saved."* Saved means preserved for everlasting *life*. We must throw off the mindset that there are things God cannot make right for those reconciled to Him, because He says otherwise.

Pray with me that God's Church will become readier to see in all things His mercy rather than His hand of judgment — for, as I

---

* Acts 2:21

say, what people interpret as God's hand of judgment, is often not from Him at all.* God sent mercy to the ancient Israelites in Egypt, and His people interpreted it as some kind of judgment. For the edification of our faith, let us examine this now.†

THE Israelites in Egypt were crying for mercy. As they cried out to God for protection and relief because they were being forced to sacrifice their newborn sons to the Nile (among other increasingly oppressive conditions), God heard their cries. And among all those innocents dying, He caused their deliverer to be born. That child grew, was educated in the ways of the cultures of his day — of the ruling class, the slave class, and then the class of tribal, desert self-sufficiency. Just when it seemed the enemy would rob their nation of a whole generation of sons, God's mercy intervened, and their deliverer was saved alive.

---

* Consider the statements made in *An Epistle on Judgment* which address issues such as this.
† Though not all things discussed here will be found in the first half of the book of Exodus, this is the general story-thread to which I refer.

Am I saying we are going to have to wait 80 years to be delivered from the crushing despotism of pharaohs of today? Not at all. I could make a very good argument that the timeline for deliverance began over 78 years ago as many were crying out for divine intervention for the sake of a generation of sons that were being sacrificed to the sea of the world.* I could also argue that we are even now within the cyclonic currents of a worldwide whirlwind.

"The LORD is slow to anger, and great in power, and will not at all acquit the wicked: the LORD hath His way in the whirlwind and in the storm, and the clouds are the dust of His feet."† And, "as the whirlwind passeth, so is the wicked no more: but the righteous is an everlasting foundation."‡

The LORD's anger has been slow to build across these past eight decades, but the whirlwind is finally here. So then must also be those deliverers He purposes to work through around this earth — and there must be more than one person, for no single

---

* Scripturally, *sea* is often symbolic of the world.

† Nahum 1:3

‡ Proverbs 10:25

person is the salvation of this whole earth except Jesus Christ our Lord. Men are just men; they are *anointed* to perform great tasks, as Moses was, by the accompanying of the power of the Holy Spirit, whether in them or on them.*

But I speak to you on God's abiding principles. In any such time of shaking, there are always men in high places, both in the darkness and in the light, who cleverly craft narratives to garner the will of the people, who are the best weapon of war for either side. Take note of whatever you find

---

* As those in Christ, we live with God's Spirit *within* us; e.g., II Corinthians 1:22—"Who hath also sealed us, and given the earnest of the Spirit *in our hearts*" (emphasis added). But in those days prior to this infilling, God's Spirit usually *came down* on those anointed to do great things. E.g., Judges 14:19—"And the Spirit of the LORD came upon him…" Thus, God can use anyone, saved or unsaved, to accomplish His purposes. His Spirit coming upon a human soul does not eradicate that soul's freedom to choose (unlike demonic possession, the goal of which is to acquire full control). If the soul cannot be in agreement with His presence and what He desires to work out through that vessel, He will leave and choose another vessel through which He can work, because there are many things He will not do without the cooperation and agreement of Man since He gave this earth to the sons of men (Psalm 115:16).

significant, and keep praying for God's Light to illuminate the truth of any matter, but current events shift and change. It is God's principles which abide forever. It is these, if we hold fast to them, which will keep us in any time of great shaking, which we observe through events contemporary to our generation.

The unprecedented nature of many events these days has startled many from their complacency. But precedented or un-precedented, no event has the power to cir-cumvent God's spiritual principles — which are always designed to work in favor toward those reconciled to Him — unless He Himself circumvents them. And I am un-convinced at this time that He ever does so. He is so perfect in strategy, methodology, and in interaction with us that He has no need to circumvent them. He designed them to allow for His intervention when necessary without compromising the integ-rity of them. Therefore it behooves us to seek to understand them.

In their school of life in ancient Egypt, the people tested poorly in their practicals (and given what we are told about them, their theory was fairly unsound too). One of the greatest mistakes the people made was in interpreting God's shaking mercy not as His kind hand extended to help them (and to help any Egyptians who would render their worship to Him rather than to false gods), but as only Pharaoh's wrath. Clearly Pharaoh became incensed at them, but it was God pressing out of Pharaoh what was already in his heart, rather than that He intended to provoke Pharaoh to anger. And really, Pharaoh did not have the power to enforce a decree against Israel that the LORD could not have countered with a simple wave of His hand. In short, the Sovereign LORD was in control the whole time, though the people chose to interpret it all as persecution by those who had power over them — and so they did have power over them, in part because the people gave it to them, even though there were many more of them than the ruling elite class.* So God labored to awaken them from this submissive complacency toward a regime that did not treat its subjects with fairness.

---

* Exodus 1:9—"And he said unto his people, Behold, the people of the children of Israel are more and mightier than we."

This divine pressing was to prepare the people to desire freedom — so the people would see Pharaoh was not the slightest bit benevolent toward them and never had been, but actually hated them, something it seems they failed to realize before the incident detailed in Exodus chapter five. It must have been like realizing someone you believed respected you for your beliefs actually looked upon you as some backwoods ignoramus. That they blamed Moses for making them a stench in Pharaoh's nostrils suggests they might have perceived him as a halfway benevolent leader somewhat sympathetic to their plight but who was also trapped by the system and could only do so much to help them. But no, it is clear they were always a stench in his nostrils and he was as eager as his ancestors to retain the slave population for the prosperity and glory of his own people, regardless what the bondage meant to the Hebrews. It was God's mercy to the people which pressed this out of him, but to the people it felt like persecution.

It seemed the people wanted relief from their burdens, but they did not truly desire freedom. God understood this and was, as gently as was possible given the situation and their disinclination to govern themselves rather than be governed, laboring to awaken them to the good plan He had for them. If He had told them everything involved in the process of delivering them from their bondage, I doubt they would have come into agreement with it.

In the days before the Lawgiver was born and grew up, the governing system over the Hebrews had been, I believe, set up to reward the people with a relatively comfortable life in exchange for obeisance to the ruling class. They arrived in Egypt in Jacob's day under the terms of shepherding Pharaoh's flocks too.* They accepted these terms gladly when they arrived because

---

* Genesis 47:6. This Pharaoh was kindly disposed toward Israel for the sake of Joseph, whom he loved as a father (Gen. 45:8). But the rulers who followed him took every advantage they could over the Hebrews. This Pharaoh likely did not discern he was setting a precedent for the people's ill-usage later, which would not be an uncommon historical occurrence—a benevolent leader followed by corrupt ones. But we also know that regardless how wicked rulers treated them later, abiding in Egypt for a time *was* God's will for them (Genesis 50:20). God fashioned preservation for Israel; He did not make men lord over Israel with evil intent. There is a great distinction between these.

there was a great famine in the land and Egypt offered supplies and protection and they were a small clan who still lived nomadically in Canaan. (That is, their hold on any land they laid claim to could be supplanted by a stronger tribe, and they could be destroyed by such an altercation.*) Pharaoh told Joseph to tell his brothers, "And take your father and your households, and come unto me: and I will give you the good of the land of Egypt, and ye shall eat the fat of the land."† Joseph's pharaoh held toward him gratitude and affection for preserving Egypt and even retaining her glory during a time of widespread, devastating famine. But after he died a new regime arose that chose not to be in remembrance of the salvation that had come from the Hebrews through one of their own.‡

---

* Consider the Shechem massacre of Genesis 34, orchestrated by Simeon and Levi, Jacob's sons. "And Jacob said to Simeon and Levi, Ye have troubled me to make me to stink among the inhabitants of the land, among the Canaanites and the Perizzites: and I being few in number, they shall gather themselves together against me, and slay me; and I shall be destroyed, I and my house" (v. 30).

† Genesis 45:18

‡ Exodus 1:8-11.

It is easy to see how at every crisis after the Exodus the first thought of many of the people was to return to Egypt, for historically it had been a place of refuge, not just for Jacob, but also for his grandfather Abraham.* They disregarded the possibility that the LORD was still working out a great deliverance for them — and that it had to take 40 whole years to complete this deliverance only because of their own sin, and not because God was not ready to accomplish it for them. Leaving Egypt was only the first phase: there also was the phase of routing the giants from the land promised to them because of their forefather Abraham's faith in God.† The final phase involved occupy-

---

* Genesis 46; 12:10-20. That things had not turned out overly well for Abraham is not entirely relevant: it is human nature to believe things will turn out better for oneself than they had for another, as evidenced by Abraham's son Isaac, who committed the same error Abraham had in Egypt but with the king of the Philistines (Genesis 26:1-11)—and Abraham committed his error *twice*, also with the ruler of the Philistines (Genesis 20).
† And because God wanted to cleanse that land of all the idolatrous blood spilled in worship to gods who lusted for the blood of Man. He was choosing to use Israel to do it for the sake of the man, Abraham, who had become His friend (James 2:23). And Abraham in turn was a descendant who worshipped Him of those to whom He had given

ing the land with such firm intent that other nations could not take it away and re-institute their bloody practices ever again. God never expected them to perform what phase three required when He first sent Moses to Egypt. Here was His mercy too: in increments was this process put in motion. "I will not drive them out from before thee in one year," said the LORD, "lest the land become desolate, and the beast of the field multiply against thee. By little and little I will drive them out from before thee, until thou be increased, and inherit the land."* God never intended that everything hap-pen overnight, and it was His mercy that did not reveal all the steps to a people who did not in their hearts wish to be an inde-pendent nation.

I am quite sure the ruling class of Egypt understood that the best way to conscript the labor of the Israelites was to give them incentives. The people clearly were fed de-cently; they obviously were not surviving at the time of the Exodus, say, on tasteless

---

His promise to someday vanquish the one who had tempted His first children (Genesis 3). One thing always leads to another....

* Exodus 23:29-30

gruel.* Their needs were evidently getting met enough that the people could continue their physically taxing menial labors, which they were still doing after the first 80 years of Moses' life.† For at the time Moses returned to Egypt, the making of bricks was still integral to the Israelites' service to the Egyptian culture.‡

But what about the long-term recompenses? Again, there is little in the biblical account to suggest anything special was done to thin the herd, so to speak, as the people began to age. Given the human sacrifices mandated to the god of the Nile around the time of Moses' birth, the Egyptians were obviously readier to cull the herd through the murder of innocents, which were probably more powerful as sacrifices to their gods anyway. Innocence usually is. So what cared they for the aged and infirm as long as they did not stick around

---

* Numbers 11:4-6

† So we can expect Egypt understood the profit that could be made from financial taxing, since clearly it understood how to physically and mentally tax persons it wished to keep in subjection to it.

‡ Exodus 5

long enough to leach wealth from their masters for their care?

Perhaps there were in place treatment options for debilitation that hastened unto death those already weakened by decades of overwork and poorer options for health and well-being such as would have been available to the elites. The people would have bought the lies (because other generations have done the same) that what they could avail themselves of was the best that could be done for pretty much any person, regardless of class. They would have been indoctrinated from birth to receive certain things as the solutions available to them, and they would not have searched beyond them because they were too tired after their labors, too comfortable after their decent meals, and too dumbed down by an educational system that was geared to training them largely to be laborers. But I believe there were long-term incentives in place as rewards for compliance and diligence because that is just how a system — an organic institution of people — runs well. Such practices probably extended further back than Egypt, and likely existed in other domineering regimes, such as the Akkadian-

Babylonian system of oppression. That is why Egypt symbolizes the world in these scriptural illustrations, because it was not as unique as it might seem at first glance. It was simply a first-world power at that time, and it was the one to which Israel — God's illustrative nation — was enslaved.

It seems the Egyptians placed Israelites as supervisors and lower-rank overlords over the masses of Hebrews; and I suspect, offered them better homes, medical care for them and their families, and higher old-age pensions if they were diligent about enforcing all the rules and regulations put on the labor class. And the labor class was all the less likely to argue these regulations when they were being forced on them by those from their own ranks. "Let there be more work laid upon the people so they have to keep working and have no time or energy or interest to listen to those who are spouting lies," and so the public officials went out and enforced the new regulations mandated by the despot on the throne.*

But what happens then? According to the Exodus paradigm, then God's manifest

---

* Exodus 5:9-10 paraphrased.

mercy to the people shows up in the form of a deliverer who has been anointed with the strength to face off against Pharaoh, the king of the world so to speak, his sorcerers, and a spiritually dull people who want him to go away; and eventually he earns the respect of the people, defeats those occult forces by God's power, and wins against the tyrannical spirit of the world. Yet in the meantime it is this class of overlords—the enforcers, the community leaders, the religious supervisors, however you want to name them—who are the first to lock arms and defend their masters' destructive agenda against the people. And why? For the sake of maintaining the status quo. For the sake of the system that has increasingly taxed them. The hard-worked people and the leaders from their ranks are more interested in life not getting worse than they are for embracing the option of it getting exponentially better.

And interestingly, the Book of Jasher—a non-canonical account of those early days—states that the Egyptians also coerced the people's hard labor *by mortaring their youngest sons in the walls* whenever they were short of bricks.* If true, this is the quality of life they wished to preserve after things were stirred up by the deliverer's arrival—a life God was mercifully laboring to deliver them from. Even if the parents would rather God removed His arm of deliverance, the blood of their children cried out to Him to be avenged of the wrong done to them.†

According to our paradigm, to whom did Moses go when he first returned to Egypt? *To the people's leadership.* It was not to rally the people. There is little or nothing to suggest Moses and Aaron embarked on

---

* Jasher 77:16-18—"And whenever any deficiency was found in the children of Israel's measure of their daily bricks, the task-masters of Pharaoh would go to the wives of the children of Israel and take infants of the children of Israel to the number of bricks deficient, they would take them by force from their mother's laps, and put them in the building instead of the bricks; whilst their fathers and mothers were crying over them and weeping when they heard the weeping voices of their infants in the wall of the building. And the task-masters prevailed over Israel, that the Israelites should place their children in the building, so that a man placed his son in the wall and put mortar over him, whilst his eyes wept over him, and his tears ran down upon his child."
† As Abel's did in Genesis 4:10. See also Revelation 6:9-11.

some great campaign to reach the people. Though rallies are wonderful for morale (and for getting news to the people without having to rely on a middleman to adjust the news according to the agenda of those to whom he may be loyal), there is a point at which they can do little more good if they are deferring the end of the war; and sometimes the war is not meant to be fought by the people. There was a battle of the titans, so to speak, and the people were carried along with it, deciding for themselves whether to side with Moses or Pharaoh, with the LORD's anointed or that little sun who was supposedly the son of the sun.* God left it to each soul to decide which leader it would stand alongside. He asked little more of them than this, except to exercise some faith in Him, the same God of their forefathers, Abraham, Isaac, and Jacob, who died in good old ages in peace.† To start it all, Moses was to speak to the Hebrew leaders per the LORD's instructions, to tell them what God was saying to them —

---

* I.e., the sun-god, Ra. The people were taught that Pharaoh was the son of the sun, the semi-deified offspring of their sun-god.

† Exodus 3:6, 15

presumably because once the leadership was on board the Deliverer-Is-Here Train, the people would also board wherever this train stopped.

Where was God's mercy for those poor, deluded souls who desperately prayed for a great deliverance from the power of those who oppressed them but who could not get the thought of Egypt out of their system, even to the point of perishing in a waste-land? Yet a whole people were saved alive and their children and grandchildren entered that promised land and had great victories against those giants. It was God's mercy to the children since He could not give it to the elders—though He stood ready to extend it to all of them. All they were asked was to exercise a little faith to believe He had mercy for them in the face of great crises—which He had already dis-played to them many times in Egypt while Pharaoh's heart was being pressed in the vise of his Creator.

In theory the Hebrew people believed the God of their fathers would hear them when they called. But in practice, when He sent a deliverer to them, they essentially de-cided their life of slavery was not so bad that they wanted their lives disrupted to the degree that their overlords were willing again to cull their numbers through violence (though they seemed willing enough to receive it through the gradual debilitation of age in an environment of hard labor and limited resources for their well-being in a land that was not known for its magnanimous care of the weak). It does appear they feared for their lives, if they were not exaggerating; because in retaliation for daring to hope for freedom for themselves, they said Pharaoh ordered his men to come after them with sword when it became necessary to set an example.[*]

Yet God fights for His victories armed with His virtues. He never needs to arm Himself with weapons of violence when it comes to dealing with His own. He has ensured through the working of His spiritual principles that all destruction against His own comes from the enemy. He saves the violence of His wrath for His enemies alone. With His love, faithfulness, peace, kindness, longsuffering, tolerance, mercy, and every other virtue in His possession,

---

[*] Exodus 5:21

He comes to rescue His own. His judgment and wrath are the last arrows He removes from His quiver and sets to His bow even with those who defy Him.

From the fourth plague to the last, Israel was exempt from being touched by the plagues, and Pharaoh was given the opportunity every time to let the Hebrews go. It was not just the Red Sea crossing that demonstrated His gracious care: it was every mercy the LORD had shown the people as He cared for them in Egypt as they awaited the finale of that battle of the titans. It was a whole gamut of mercies they were failing to remember, not just one big mercy at the end. And if they could not bring themselves to be in remembrance of what God had done directly for them, how could they be expected to pass onto their children remembrance of it?

I earnestly believe many of those men who perished in the wilderness passed into Paradise upon dying. Decades later they had finally learned the lesson of surrender to the God who continually cared for them the rest of their days (though it seemed they still could not keep from grumbling, which many of us can easily understand). It was just that the LORD could not reward them with life in the promised land for behavior that failed to establish the rock-hard fortitude the next generation needed upon entering it themselves. He wanted to extend mercy to all, but in the end He had to settle for extending it to the generations following because the older ones would not come into agreement with His plans to conquer the giants of the land. It is clear they would have made themselves subservient to a new regime for the sake of being cared for as they had in Egypt, choosing to overlook the fact that in this low quality of care there was not much to defend. And instead of cleansing that land from the practice of human sacrifice, they would have all the sooner partaken of it (as they did later and so were judged and sent into exile*). We are frankly told — another one of those hard truths we are expected to reconcile within us — that the children had to suffer for decades for the sins of the parents.†

---

* Jeremiah 7:30-8:3; 9:12-16, 25-26 (regarding vv. 25-26—only the spiritually circumcised, those in spiritual covenant with God, can escape a judgment that overtakes the powers of the world).
† Numbers 14:33

God resorts to punishment, consequences for our choices, when we have refused to listen many times to the warnings He has sent, or when after many opportunities to be moved, we refuse to submit to the conscience He has placed in us. It took a number of trials before He consigned those elders to graves in the desert for the sake of the spiritual well-being of their children. Again, He would have preferred to show mercy to the young and the old, but in the end He was only able to show it to the young, because of their own free will the old would not choose to believe that at their age there still might be something better beyond the life they had known in Egypt. Yet from the witness of Joshua and Caleb, the blessing of a promised land is not barred from the older generations. In truth, the older person's willingness to embrace change seems to have its roots in earlier years. But according to our paradigm, less of them stand up eagerly to take hold of it than do those who chant against them.* I am

---

* And we see from Numbers 13-14 that the seeds of this rejection of the promises does not start at 80: that is, their faith was not put on trial at 60, 70, 80—those decades when people are more likely to

not consigning any generation to a certain fate. I am simply highlighting what our paradigm for such times teaches us.

Let us try our best not to judge who is worthy of God's mercy and who is not. But let us also not fail to believe in God's mercy, and to respond to it. It may very well provoke occurrences we really do not want to deal with—such as the elders' agreement with the LORD's words from Moses provoked Pharaoh's ire and the subsequent plagues—but I tell you the truth, God's mercy *is* real. Sometimes it is hard to discern through the overall process of deliverance, but it will not fail to live up to the paradigm He preserved for us throughout history.

---

declare they are too old for change. We know this because in God's judgment of Numbers 14—and God is always eminently fair—He consigned every male "from twenty years old and upward, which have murmured against Me" (v. 29). We plant seeds of disbelief from youth; and so from youth we must make a concerted effort to sow seeds of a degree of faith that delivers us into a promised land.

EVERY time the people had a victory, the enemy (those Egyptian elites bent on death and destruction so they could add to their wealth and power with the help of their slave force) tried to make the people pay many-fold for the simple defiance of believing a good report over an evil one (e.g., that they belonged to the LORD to set them free over that they belonged to Pharaoh to do with as he pleased), or because they ceased to grovel before corrupt leadership (which is the prerequisite to all overlording it seems). That the rule of a few over many does not succeed in all its efforts BECAUSE OF THE LORD'S MERCY, is the only reason we are still warring for good today. For if the enemies of God felt they could have achieved their goals by now, they would have. This earth would already have been scorched and its population decimated so that its resources would not be wasted on useless eaters. But strategy after strategy has ultimately failed to accomplish across history the total subjugation of the masses to those who would rule over them. And whether or not people attribute this to God's merciful sovereignty does not alter the truth that this is the force behind Man's preservation.

The account suggests that whenever the slavery might become just too much for the people to remain healthy and active enough to accomplish their labors, it was kept in check by various aids. They had decent food supplied to them as we have seen, and it is likely they had opportunity to buy more resources from time to time. "You are tired, have aches and pains? Here are remedies I will sell you so that you will feel better" — understanding that the greater health will go toward sustaining the oppressive economy — more coins in the pocket for odd labors done for benevolent patrons then go back into this economy by the purchasing of better food and herbs that will keep the people as well as possible so they can perform their labors, and so on and so forth without end.

Here we see that their Egyptian masters arranged through the orderly working of their economic system to have straw delivered for the bricks they must make. After the deliverer arrives they are told to gather their own. And instead of seeing this as the next merciful step in driving Pharaoh to his utter ruin, they blame the deliverer for provoking Pharaoh's wrath against them. And how do we know they ought to have exercised faith over fear? We know because Moses took this difficulty to the LORD and inquired why it had occurred. And the LORD answered him and directed him to give His words to the people.* "And Moses spake so unto the children of Israel: but they hearkened not unto Moses for anguish of spirit, and for cruel bondage."†

The Israelites were certainly pressed, and of course we can understand their feeling. It is probably comparable to a government-employed road crew being told they won't get paid for their work without providing out of pocket the concrete necessary for their labors. The Hebrews were largely making the bricks for the constant Egyptian construction, and then they get told they have to furnish some of their own supplies or there would be retribution for failing to fulfill their quotas. It requires real faith to believe in God's mercy at such times, but neither does there seem to be an

---

* Exodus 5:22-6:8

† Exodus 6:9

alternative if one wishes the bondage to cease.

God in His mercy sent a deliverer to Egypt, and one of the first things that happened was that the regular system was disrupted. And the next thing that happened was oppression. Yet the words the LORD had given Moses to pass along to the Hebrew leadership were a warning — a word of preparation for their hearts — that Pharaoh's heart would turn hard in response to God's mercy being worked out for the people *before he would let them go*.

Their enemy attempted to oppress in response to every small victory — even the initial victory of simply receiving by faith words of deliverance. Jesus taught us that "when any one heareth the word of the kingdom, and understandeth it not, then cometh the wicked one, and catcheth away that which was sown in his heart."* What did the Hebrew elders do in response to Moses' first visit, when he showed them the LORD's signs? They heard what he had to say and believed him so much they *bowed*

---

* Matthew 13:19

*their heads and worshipped.** But as Jesus essentially told us, we have to hold onto words we do not understand with an extra firm grip because it is those the enemy most particularly comes to steal away. Perhaps because they are the easiest to grab: those we understand get planted in the soil of the soul, beneath the dark earth. They put down roots and continue to germinate before the plant appears above the earth and bears fruit. But those that do not get planted lie on top of the earth where the birds come to pluck them away. And while we are still here, what we understand is far less than what we believe we understand. That is one of the reasons God implores us to exercise our faith, because He knows just how much we do not understand about what is at stake.

Does God ever ask more of us than He has those who illustrated His paradigms? No, I do not believe so, not generally speaking, for they were chosen *because* they were like us.† As long as we respond with faith and prayerful worship, He will continue

---

* Exodus 4:30-31

† E.g., James 5:17

with His labor of delivering us—from whatever oppresses us—and He might continue even without it if He has appointed deliverance to happen at that time because of a word He gave one of His friends long before. I say this because in the first Exodus God set Israel free because of His promise to Abraham as much as because of His compassion on the people. So even if the people had not come into agreement with His words, He still had to arrange their emancipation in order to keep His promise to His friend Abraham. If He had not freed them, His promise to His friend would have gone unfulfilled.

Some blessings are conditional, such as scriptural promises dependent on a personal response. We can nullify their fulfillment if we are not walking in obedience to God's standard for our life. Our failure to receive them does not hinder others' success in receiving them. But other things are fulfilled because the blessing hearkens back beyond our little lives. In short, sometimes it is all part of a much bigger picture than what we are willing to do or not do. In these cases it is why nothing can stop what God in battle array sets out to bring to pass against those who oppress His own. It was why all who partook of the blessing had to go together if they went at all, because the blessing was for the whole people, for them to be set up as their own nation with their own system of self-governance. It was not conditioned on any single person's acceptance or rejection of it. Not to partake of this kind of corporate blessing means staying behind in Egypt. There was no way to set up a new way of independent life for them in their own country and partake of this by those who refused to leave whatever sanctuary Egypt could afford them. So where one of the emancipated people went, all went. Not to go meant not being emancipated from the old system.

The Hebrew leadership's later response of what they were unwilling to do when they told Moses to go away and leave them alone could not nullify God's promise to Abraham's descendants. But neither did God's fulfillment of the Abrahamic promise force any soul from Egypt who did not wish to go. God mercifully ignored this later response of a few men for the sake of a whole people, practically speaking, and chose not to deviate from the covenant they solidified through their initial act of faith, even though in that first act He was using the voices of a few to solidify the commitment of the whole people. He mercifully understood that they could not perceive the bigger picture.* But whether all those men left Egypt, we do not know. Their personal choices had the power to nullify the practical outworking of the Abrahamic promise in their life. Interestingly, we are not told the number of elders Moses and Aaron brought together when they first arrived in Egypt to deliver the LORD's message. We are told by the time they got to Sinai that this number was seventy.† But perhaps it had been much greater in Egypt, but only seventy chose to leave.

Do not forget that while those leaders made it through the Red Sea, they then died in the wilderness. I do not want to be one of those who lived to see an Exodus, should I be so privileged to do so, but who then was unable to come into a blessed life in the promised land. Do you? How tragic that

---

* As if God was essentially saying, "Too late. The blessing is already on its way. The only way you can avoid it is to refuse to be swept along with it."
† Exodus 24:1, 9

they could not find the courage to take the land the LORD promised them was already theirs. I understand their fear. But I cannot change the paradigm, which is based on how things work when God is ready to intervene: there are giants in the land. Yet the God who sent the blood, the boils, the darkness, the death, and who parted the Red Sea, is still big enough to get His people through any new application of this biblical paradigm.

God's people are not required to part their Red Sea or to take out their Egyptians: that battle is always the LORD's according to the paradigm. He fights for the people, and the people hold their peace.* Israel did not have to fight Egypt with physical weapons; they did not have to fight Egypt at all. They had to in faith persevere in Goshen as they awaited the climax of the battle of the titans. They did later have to fight the giants who occupied the high places in the

---

* Exodus 14:13-14; and what is the believer's peace? "And His name shall be called Wonderful Counsellor, The mighty God, The everlasting Father, The Prince of Peace" (Isaiah 9:6). It is to our Prince of Peace we hold fast when the battle rages and the glory of the LORD is about to be seen.

land which they had been promised. In Egypt they merely had to come into agreement with the LORD's words for their deliverance and prepare themselves for a great move. For His part, God continued to shake everything that could be shaken, and unfortunately He had to do so until there was little left of a once glorious nation.

I am sometimes bothered by the thought that if the Hebrew leaders had backed the one sent to them to help, it could have all been over much sooner, because God did not give Moses an exact number of plagues it would take before the people would be set free, just that He would display His power through many wonders.* Ten plagues suggests that God judged Egypt in a comprehensive way. But that no number was given to Moses beforehand suggests that if a lesser judgment could have effected Israel's deliverance, God would have utilized it. That He knew ten would be required — a complete act of judgment — is not entirely the point: in the legal annals of Heaven, it will be known for all time that the Great High Judge on His Bench had to

* Exodus 3:20; 6:1

resort to utilizing all ten before Egypt's grasp was shaken loose from its hold on His people.*

God had to keep shaking Egypt because either Egypt would not let go, or His own people refused to do so. Their primary goal was in appeasing the throne-thug so they could get past the disruptions and life would return to normal. Sure it might be a little disappointing for a while after hearing such huge words about a great deliverance and then not having one, especially since they had been praying for one for decades. But is it really worth all this? Is it worth the wrath of Pharoah? "His men have lethal weapons, Lord, and they are fully willing to use them against us!"

I think this is perhaps why the Exodus paradigm does not provide us with exact

---

* In any judgment of such degree, I would guess that God ensured the number of ten afflictions because it symbolized the completeness of the act. That is, He adjusted His plagues accordingly so that by the time He got to the tenth, if indeed ten would be necessary, the judgment would be complete and the battle won. His battle strategy is perfect—well above and beyond what some refer to as multidimensional chess.

timing—because the event itself was not dependent on it. I think the event of leaving Egypt was perhaps as dependent on the people's willingness to walk away from their slavery as it was dependent on demonstrating to them that Pharaoh would never treat them better while in Egypt. If the people had demonstrated more of an unwillingness to keep sustaining the regular order of the nation's system, I do not believe Pharaoh could have continued his opposition as long as he did. It took as long as it did to complete the process of deliverance because God was mercifully waiting on His people to come into agreement about leaving their life of slavery as much as He was keeping open the window of repentance for Pharaoh and the Egyptians.

To the Hebrews it probably seemed they would never leave, and to the Egyptians it probably seemed the plagues would never end. But God acted with mercy—unleashing one plague at a time and ever ready to conclude the business should Pharaoh give the word and let His people go. And with this He was balancing the people's preparation for desiring to become an independent nation, which centuries in Egypt had beaten out of them. But He was unwilling to take them forth without their agreement to become independent. God labored to keep all these factors balanced until deliverance absolutely had to occur to avoid the violence the hard-pressed tyrant sought to invoke against a people who were defying his heavy-handed regime. And whether it looked like the oppressor was getting by with a lot of his ill-will toward the people, such as what happened in Exodus 5, well, God never lost sight of the truth that He was bearing them hence "as a man doth bear his son."[*]

That the Egyptians desired to keep their labor force was unarguable. Their economy was built around the Israelites carrying the burden of much of the manual labor. But for sure the battle was the LORD's, and He can save a nation in a day.[†] In order for it all

---

[*] Deuteronomy 1:31

[†] Zechariah 3:9—"For behold the stone that I have laid before Joshua; upon one stone shall be seven eyes: behold, I will engrave the graving thereof, saith the LORD of hosts, and I will remove the iniquity of that land in one day." This was supremely fulfilled on Good Friday, that day Jesus died in atonement for the sins of the people. But God is at liberty to use His Word in other applications. These applications do not refute the

to have happened faster than it did, God required unity between His anointed and the people's leadership, because this man was not merely the one who interceded to Pharaoh: he was to be the one who, as a shepherd, would lead the people as a giant flock. Even so, it was less imperative that Moses' agreement as the LORD's mouthpiece be with the people, because practically speaking, people are generally willing to back who their leadership backs, provided they respect their leaders. God's mercy *was* being worked out for their nation, but what they most felt was the extended oppression that erupted due to divine shaking across that land. That one day of a Great Change seemed further off with every plague, I am sure. Yet our paradigm illustrates to us that for His part God had no intention of leaving undone what He of His own free will had started.

Egypt demonstrated that it was willing to take many lives in order to achieve its goals of keeping the Hebrews dominated to its own luxury, glory, and power. The

---

original context; they illustrate the eternality of the Word.

plague against the Egyptian firstborn came because Pharaoh threatened Moses, Israel's firstborn, so to speak — and firstborn in the sense that he was of that group of sons cast into the Nile — the firstborn of those who were by divine decree destined for freedom. He was a type, a representation, of the firstborn sons of God's eldest son, Israel. And he was a symbolic firstborn as the primary leader for his people. Egypt violently took the lives of many Hebrew sons in its effort to keep the people subjected to its rule, and so the LORD took theirs in repayment because the Law for Man is "life for life."*

The old covenant based on the blood of beasts can only be superseded by the New Covenant which is based on Christ's Blood, which at that time was not yet in effect. For those who will not be brought under the

---

* Exodus 21:23. Should we be surprised to someday learn that the number of Egyptians which died in the last plague exactly matched the number of Hebrew sons cast into the Nile? —or that this number matched all the wrongful deaths accumulated over the generations of Egypt's abusive exercise of authority? The only things God forgets is what the Covenant's Blood covers from His sight.

covering Blood of Christ, they must be judged then by the old law of retribution. This is the principle of God's laws for judgment and mercy. I pray that as long as these laws endure, many more will experience His mercy than who have to receive His judgment. If you are ever concerned as to what you deserve in judgment, plead the Blood of Christ; for if you do deserve some kind of retribution, you will fall under the law of it unless you take to yourself the covering Blood.

When Pharaoh decreed the death of Moses, Israel's firstborn, God flipped around the tables and instead required blood from the ruling class as retribution for the life extinguished of Abraham's sons. And He had the power to enforce this just judgment. Instead of an Egyptian priest holding a knife over a form bound on its altars of power, wealth, and fertility, the LORD effectually put the knife into the strong grasp of His reaper angel, turned the idolatrous altar around so the celebrants could not raise their eyes to their false gods, and He bound them to their own stone, bloodied by the bodies of many slaves.

Was this unjust of God? Was this unmerciful to one that He might be merciful to another, as though God shows favoritism?* But if Pharaoh had not hardened his heart and had been willing to show mercy himself to a people who had given centuries of labor without due recompense, the LORD would not have had to accomplish such great wonders to free them. Because for all His power, God is never gratuitous. He never shows off without cause (though in Heaven I believe He performs many things for the simple enjoyment of His children, such as fireworks displays). God manifested His mercy to the Hebrews at the expense of the Egyptians, but we must not forget that Egypt took many Hebrew lives, especially 80 years prior to their deliverance.

From Man's eyes Pharaoh's mandate of the death of the infant sons might appear to be primarily a part of a conflict between nations, with the stronger one willing to do what was necessary to sustain its power; and during such conflicts, there are casual-

---

* Romans 2:11—"For there is no respect of persons with God."

ties. It is to be expected. Just as it ought to be expected that nations war against nations. This is what people are taught. But those most loyal to their gods understand that these gods are much more satisfied with the blood of many young men.

For God's first created and beloved son was a man. In Adam those who rebelled in Heaven saw God's love for a blood-filled man (which must have appeared weaker than their light-filled forms) whose innocence of wrongdoing highlighted their own rebellion every instant. So they still seek to obtain through their place holders the spilling of the blood of other young men, and the more innocent the blood spilled, the more satisfied they are by it (though never fully appeased, which is why they always thirst for more).

These entities like Man to believe it is the wrath the gods have against him (as though this is the natural relationship between deity and human), but this is mostly a lie. It is the fallen ones' wrath against God, who placed His glory and affection on those they deemed far lesser in quality than themselves. They were insulted, simply put. And so they take out their wrath against God on us. The easiest way to spill this blood is to convince the people it is somehow in their best interest to sacrifice their sons. In this case they were essentially told, "It's you and the rest of your family or your sons." So they sent their sons to their deaths. I am sure it was not just to the god of the Nile they sacrificed them. Were any of Egypt's wars against other people fought using Hebrew slaves as their armed forces? And how many of the Hebrew underlords were kept in line by coercing them through threat to their sons? It is very sad that so many have joined the bloody cause of those set against God, even to the loss of the life of their soul.

Our study of Israel's history is incomplete, whether in Egypt or out of it. There are many other points that could be made. Let us revisit this subject at a later time. I pray you can discern in my letter all those parallels you might be able to make in your present life, and to be strengthened by the ancient account so that God can use your agreement with His ways to accomplish as much as He can for you.

Many of our questions seem straightforward in theory, and it is a relatively simple exercise to study a paradigm and pick out parallels, even if at first not always easy. But in practice, things can manifest much darker than the people expect. It is God's mercy too that does not provide all the details until we have to have them. The testing of our faith often appears unexpectedly, and we can become disheartened by it. I know from my own experience there are things I would rather not have learned before I did, because knowing myself, I realized I could not have borne the truth with equanimity until deliverance came. And sometimes deliverance is not dependent on just what I want for my life or what God wants for my life. It is dependent on a bigger picture than just the one of my little sphere, or it is dependent on more than just myself within that sphere. And God is asking me to come into agreement with what He wants for my whole sphere of influence, His whole Church, or for all the oppressed peoples involved. You are weary of the testing of your faith, I know, but take to heart the spiritual knowledge revealed to us in His Word that He *will* finish what He started by His own initiative — His own initiative began the great work, and by His own continuing initiative, it will be finished.

LET me leave you with these thoughts:

Before Jesus won back the keys to death and hell, the devil held them within his domain—this consisting of death, darkness, and hell*. God did not circumvent this shifting of authority after Adam's generation (as though Adam's going to the grave would have justified enough time to take

---

* The nether land of the grave is a bit iffy, as though it is a temporary place for the soul, which is required to pass on to either eternal Life or eternal death. The devil may not have purview over the grave, but neither, it seems, can a soul decide to remain in the grave and be able to enforce this with its own power if it does not wish to be taken into God's Home. The grave's boundaries seem to be the moment of death until it must pass through to either Heaven or hell, and I would not want to bank on the soul's stay there being longer than it might turn out to be. The only real security is in receiving eternal Life through the sealing Blood of Jesus Christ during this life. It also seems that grave-grace may be dependent on whether someone is praying for you to have it; and I shudder to think of all those unlikeable persons for whom no one wants to pray or even think about. For believers there is, practically speaking, no grave. In effect, they bypass it: "O death, where is thy sting? O grave, where is thy victory?" (I Cor. 15:55—note that the number five, tripled here, is a number symbolic of grace).

back these keys for his descendants that appeared innocent of his sin; in short, as though Man had suffered long enough). This authority remained in place those thousands of years until our Lord's death and resurrection. Instead, He established for Adam and his righteous seed a place later called Abraham's Bosom.* Its other name was *Paradise.* And so it was for them. And where did God establish this land for them? *IN HELL.*

Paradise, where the righteous in God's sight rested until the fullness of time arrived for the fulfillment of the sacrificial act needed to reconcile Man to God, was placed in Hades, which we are taught was the abode of the dead, both of the wicked and the righteous before the Blood of Christ was shed for the remission of sin and those souls could be transformed into the mettle of Christ's Essence so that they could dwell with the Consuming Fire and not be consumed by it. Because it was not the Heaven we know of today, and because it still seems to be the place where souls go who do not enter Heaven, we can refer to Hades

---

* Luke 16:19-31

as hell. There are distinctions, but for our purpose here, it was hell in the sense that souls did not yet dwell with God in His Home; rather, He fashioned a temporary home for the righteous soul in the same locality as the one that housed the unrighteous. With only a great gulf dividing the abode of these righteous and the wicked, the souls of the righteous lived in conditions of paradise while they awaited that Great Day. And they did so in open sight of those who had died unrepentant of their sins and existed under the authority of the one whose kingdom is only one of death, darkness, and torment. Pretty cool, huh?

I do not want to experience hell, and I do not wish to have it in sight. I have no desire to see in torment even the most heinous sinner, or to have them in their torment looking always on my paradise. I choose to come into agreement with God's Word that some will go to hell because I believe He gives us the Truth.* I cannot subscribe to a belief in universalism merely because I wish it were so if this is not part of God's

---

* That some will end up in hell, see for example, Matthew 5:30.

Truth. But that God created a paradise for His people in the very depths of hell — well, I find that extremely comforting. It is one of the great illustrations that God does not show favoritism: He made no distinction between those righteous and unrighteous before the fullness of time had come to enact the Great Sacrifice of His Son's Atonement, which brought with it the Great Transformation of Man's Soul. Every one of them had to await that time in depths of the earth according to the judgment He had given Adam.* Even so, some lived in paradise.

---

* Genesis 3:19; but however you want to interpret such verses as applying only to the body returning to the earth, the truth of a place separate from the Heaven we think of today was clearly taught us by Jesus Himself in His parable of Luke 16:19-31 of the rich man and Lazarus, which we know is not the Heaven of today because by all accounts today's Heaven is not visible to hell and vice versa. Jesus was likening His message of contrasting destinies to the belief system of the afterlife to which they held; and if He was using something that was not really true as the framework for His parable, it would be the only place in the gospel accounts He did so. Whether the Jewish culture held beliefs that were not really true (as all cultures do), is not being argued. That Jesus always chose to speak from a framework of what *was* true and to ignore false beliefs in His use of parables in His teaching, is what I am saying.

We tend to conclude that being near hell must have diluted the quality of paradise, though if you force the question, your respondents might answer differently since they were required to consider the matter. Those who dwelt in Paradise were not touched by the hellish conditions across that great gulf. That's the point. Just because something is in sight does not mean we will be touched by it. Was Israel touched by (most of) the plagues in Goshen? And since the physical instructs us in the spiritual, is not there a spiritual Goshen for us that God's people reside in? Does not His Word promise that here, in the habitation of the secret place of the most High, "shall no evil befall thee, neither shall any plague come nigh thy dwelling"?* And regarding why the people had to partake of the first three plagues, does not the soul customarily require a few trials before it is able to put into practice invisible principles of preservation?

We should never rejoice that hell is filled, if it will be. I would much rather those caverns echoed with silence because

---

the most monstruous sinners received God's mercy and were now in Heaven with the ranks of the reconciled, than I would to receive the news justice had been served. After all, what are the sins of one lifetime compared with an eternity of torment? (— though I am not questioning God's judgments.) God has set the boundaries around one lifetime as the period in which Man's will shall be tested; and God's tests are eminently fair. We have to choose, as each soul does, to come into agreement or not with God's Word for us. We are not required to understand all of it, just the part that there must be a Mediator between our soul and God — and we really do not *have* to understand this either: we just have to be humble enough to accept it as the Truth of Man's spiritual state and to submit our soul to the Way of Christ for our salvation. Does a small child ever have to understand why it must not touch a hot stove? It will understand by and by; presently, for its salvation from harm, it just has to obey.

The hardest truth to accept about deliverance is that not everyone will receive it. There are some who will suffer here (or live it up here, as the rich man in Jesus' parable did), and then they will suffer in hell forever. It is a complex subject — why people go to hell — and not our primary one here. But every day God permits the sinner to continue is another day that person has to reconsider his way and to repent. Every day is another day of mercy for that soul so that it may undergo the greatest deliverance of all: freedom from the bondage of sin. For those set against God, I say in Jesus' Name, feel the fear of the One who has the power to destroy both body and soul in hell,* and then decide whether you will be for Him or against Him.

After all, we don't necessarily have to like the one with whom we choose to side; we just wisely realize we would be better off siding with that person for whatever reason. For some people it is like that in the choice between God and the devil. A soul can't win — won't ever win — by siding with the one who was already defeated long ago. If he could not defeat God in two thousand more years, having had thousands prior to that since Adam fell, he is not going to now. And frankly, there are many souls who feel

---

* Matthew 10:28

they do not like God much, but they don't want to go to hell either. So they are obligated to weigh the matter; and if they feel they can accept God on His terms to avoid hell, they will. It is almost a childlike trust they exercise in an invisible God who defeated an invisible devil, accepting it all as real with the state of their soul at stake. Yet God would have all His children grow up to be spiritual men even while retaining the childlike faith that has utter trust in its Caregiver.

I would much rather Jesus had ended His parable with the rich man and his brothers lying in Abraham's Bosom alongside Lazarus; but He was unable to finish His story this way. Why? Because, I believe, the rich man knew in his heart there was no true repentance. And in his heart he could not say there ever would have been since he felt his misery while seemingly not ashamed for having failed to do right by God and neighbor. He asked for Lazarus' help because Lazarus might have been the only soul he could see across the gulf whom he had known on earth; we don't know that he had any confession to make. Jesus chose to craft His story without one, which signifies something to me. It seems he knew in his heart that there was nothing in Heaven, hell, or earth that would have kept him from his selfish pleasures. The torment of hell made him miserable, and the only affection he had was for his brothers who were as reprobate as he had been. Even sinners have their affections, so we cannot conclude sincere repentance for his wrong-doings was involved in his request that Lazarus be sent to his brothers to keep them from hell.

Jesus understood that if people will not receive God's words and the servants He sends to help us apply His eternal Word to our day and circumstances (which are His prophets), they also will not respond to the Truth of God's Life should someone rise from the dead in living illustration of that Life His servants have been laboring to speak about to the people. –because they do not care about that Life: they care only about their own. They know that they would have still chosen to indulge them-selves in whatever way they wanted to go, regardless of statements made against doing these things or any demonstration of what heavenly Life can do — again, because it is not this Life they are interested in.[*]

But for all those thousands of years, the devil had in hand those powerful keys. Though only God is indestructible Life, fallen Lucifer had the power to lock and unlock certain doors. Did he use those keys on behalf of servants favored for their deeds for his kingdom? (—and not because he loved them, but because it was good propaganda to reward those faithful to him.) Did he perhaps lock doors against righteous enemies coming in retribution against his servants, thus staving off deaths that would have occurred at that time? Or did he open doors so that death would be released against his servants' enemies? And did he convince himself of his utter power over Man during those centuries when God waited for bowls of iniquity to fill?

God's Word teaches us that Jesus now holds these keys[†] — this is part of the theory

---

[*] This is not precisely the same thing as the way, say, an addiction robs (or at least strongly hinders) someone of free choice and binds them to looking primarily at self. In every soul God searches for intent of heart, and He judges accordingly.
[†] Revelation 1:18

of our faith. But practically we live as though they are still in the unmerciful possession of the devil who actively labors to lock and unlock in favor of his servants and against the righteous ones of God. Yet only God can gift eternal Life, and the devil no longer has possession of the keys to death and hell. Let us endeavor to remember this truth and to declare that God has mercifully made His Life our portion.

It is arguable that Hades became known as hell because God had abandoned it after removing from the abode of the dead all those souls willing to be reconciled to Him. So let us trust that wherever we are with God, He desires to make into a paradise for us.

You are well on your way to spiritual manhood, or you would not be reading this letter. Do not give up. Do not believe the enemy's lies that you are still childish and worthy of much discipline. Accept what discipline that comes, but accept it from the hand of the Father who loves you and wants to bless you as much as He can, and your children after you. Do not be one of those toward whom He had to make a distinction between them and their children.

Let us not be like those grumblers He had to let die in the wilderness for the sake of their children — their *deaths* were the blessing the children awaited so that they would be released to enter the promised land. By God's grace may we never be such a blessing as that to those in our sphere of influence. Let us be of one mind and spirit and so all receive His mercy of a blessed life. And keep looking up. It is the enemy's afflictions that are intended never to end; God the Father always places boundaries on His chastisement of His children.

YOU were chosen for this time. God has a purpose for you. He did not send you here just so the devil could have at you. It is written: "Mark the perfect man, and behold the upright: for the end of that man is peace. But the transgressors shall be destroyed together: the end of the wicked shall be cut off. But the salvation of the righteous is of the LORD: He is their strength in the time of trouble. And the LORD shall help them, and deliver them: He shall deliver them from the wicked, and save them, because they trust in Him.'"*

Every soul, regardless of when or how it dies — because this is the end of a righteous man even after he is saved from many troubles in this life — is subject to this principle that those reconciled to God are raised to eternal Life. This is a divine principle we can bank on. God's mercy will not be defeated for those with whom He no longer has any quarrel. The devil takes credit for many deaths, and so he does steal away many persons' lives prematurely, but this is also his propagandist efforts toward those of us here on earth — for everyone in the spiritual realms knows that he hasn't won anything for those who are reconciled to God. Everyone knows in the spiritual realms that the points go to God no matter how or when those persons died. They have been saved unto everlasting Life and are forever beyond his reach.

I never want to become desensitized to souls not yet reconciled to God, or to people dying through what appear to be calamitous ends. Any day could be the final day

---

* Psalm 37:37-40

for those unreconciled, particularly since they do not claim the protection of the Blood of Jesus and this may leave them vulnerable at any time for the thieving spirits of death, destruction, and debilitation to reach them. So I pray that every soul passing into death must face Jesus, who is the Gate to Heaven, but who also holds the keys to death and hell.

I have respectfully bidden the Lord to keep the doors of death and hell locked until souls face Him one last time. This is the final mercy I can invoke for them, and I earnestly hope I do so rightly. Often a soul has seared its conscience against Him, and it will not listen to any amount of entreaties here. But there, in that nebulous no-man's land between Heaven and hell, with Heaven's gates open above and joyful sounds and ethereal lights emanating from beyond; and the sounds of torment, the stench of death, and the sensation of scorching heat below, perhaps the years of hard-hearted defiance will fade away and some remembrance of those early years of trust will return — before evil disillusioned them of the reality that goodness does exist and it is greater than evil. So I declare that they

MUST face one last time the One who holds the keys. They must face Him because He holds the keys and I have locked the door to hell in His Name and, I earnestly hope, by His authority. So they cannot just pass on through it without asking Him to open it for them.

They also cannot pass into Heaven without choosing to be reconciled to God through Him, for Jesus is the Father's Emissary; but, as I said, perhaps in those moments, severed from hindering flesh and soul-wounding earth, they can see something in His expression they once saw in childhood, in a Man they heard about in stories, or One they thought existed but whose existence seemed increasingly remote as they grew older. They MUST ask Him to open the heavy door to hell so that they can pass through, because if a soul could open those doors of its own strength, the keys would be useless.

They cannot avoid hell by saying nothing, for Jesus is the Truth; and those who face Him are bound to reveal the truth of their life to the Truth who was made Lord over us all. They must choose either Heaven or hell; and if hell, then they must ask of their own free will that He unlock the door for them with His key. And He will. He will not force any soul to dwell in Heaven if they cannot stand to be in the presence of God. Though it will grieve Him to see them go, the Father will not allow them to pass through those pearly gates if they do not intend to live in peace with His children. Never again will He suffer the likes of prideful Lucifer in His heavenly Kingdom. But of their own free will — there will be absolutely no mistake about this — will they pass through, because they either have to say the words, "I demand you unlock for me the door to hell," or in saying nothing in the hope of avoiding just judgment, God will weigh their soul on His scales, and that verdict shall decide. And I would rather trust God's verdicts than Man's (or the devil's). If His scales demonstrate a soul weighed in on the hell side and that soul does not wish to be reconciled, then I accept that. I accept that this soul will go to hell for all eternity, dying again and again and again in torment forever.

God does not make hell a place of torment. Those who are filled with hatred for one another do so. Basically it is a place where entities get their kicks out of hurting one another; and since the soul is eternal, they are able to do it forever. The one with more power will always win. So no human soul will ever accumulate more power than that which is demonic—because the true source of a soul's power is God. That power of self it may have nurtured to great strength in this world will not avail it now, for it is nothing once being disconnected from the earth by which Man was made.

This is how God designed Man: created of the earth to have loving dominion over it, and created of God so that once having finished his purposes on earth, he could be translated into his heavenly Home. Hell was designed for the rebellious angels, and so it was not designed as a place in which Man would find blessing. If Man will not choose the blessing of spiritual salvation on earth for the destiny of eternal salvation in Heaven, there is no other place for his soul to find a home, because in hell there is no access to the power God desired Man's soul to have. This is why souls eternally die in torment, because those who were originally consigned to hell gleefully exercise their power over those who were successfully robbed of the inner power God joyfully created them to possess. Many souls let pride of life burgeon in their self until their arrogance is virtually limitless. They feel empowered by their bitterness toward Father, Son, and Holy Spirit. I pray too that in these days God utilizes the one thing that makes eternal death and hell real to them so that they might exercise humbleness before the only One that can save their soul.

From our vantage point we see much death — both in the time of the judgments of Egypt but also after the people came out to journey to their promised land — and it is only through the eyes of faith that we can see higher when this paradigm again comes into play. Again, God's mercy stands ready to come to every soul who calls upon the Name of Jesus to be saved: "And it shall come to pass, that whosoever shall call on the name of the Lord shall be saved."*

It is a hard truth that God will permit suffering if that is the only thing remaining to awaken that soul to raise its gaze to Him and to cry out for deliverance, and this too is His mercy, for it is the eternal destiny of

---

* Acts 2:21

the soul at stake. Israel cried out to be delivered from Egypt for their material well-being, and God heard them and freed them. But for His part, God never forgets that it is for spiritual well-being souls must be freed from their bondage to sin. He wants to give us both kinds of freedom, just as He wanted to show mercy to both the older generation and the young after bringing them forth from their slavery.

God asks us to trust in His mercy regardless what things look like because He promises us it is everlasting. It endures forever. He asks us to raise our gaze as soon as we are able, given grief and responsibilities, to replace images of death with ones of life. He does not expect us to repress or to deny the deaths of those around us. But neither does He want us to accept that we have to be subjected to the power of it because we have called on His Name to be saved, or those who died have. It is a matter of principle to save those who call on Him in sincerity and in truth. As difficult as it is to process death, especially when violence is involved, it is not the end. We do not always have to understand why certain things occur; and even if He is willing to explain, if it is a time of purification of our faith — the testing of the fiery furnace — He cannot explain why or it would not be a true test of what we have endeavored to learn. In His mercy He will take us through the trial as quickly as He can, given the big picture, the others involved, and how willing we are to remain in agreement with His word of deliverance for us.

Let us pray together:

God of all souls, have mercy upon the innocent sufferer and the unrepentant wicked, by whose hands these innocents often die. We declare with You to the enemy, YOU SHALL NOT PASS HERE IN THE SHADOW OF THE WINGS OF SHADDAI, our holy Lord and divine protector, according to the great promises given to us in Psalm 91.

By the Blood of our precious Lord Jesus, let there be Life, Light, and Love in the land of Man from now until the catching away. Let not the Lord's great Sacrifice be in vain wherever it can accomplish its work. Let Thy mercy fall upon this earth, but also Thy judgment come against those who will not cease to oppress and murder the innocent, since there was no other way to reach them but by Thy judgment. And having experienced Thy judgment, what will be left to *them but Thy mercy? For it is written that Thine "anger endureth but a moment."* What other weapons wilt Thou pull from Thy quiver but Thy love and mercy and all Thy virtues which are everlasting, once Thine anger has been satisfied?*

Give them the mercy of whatever time You can, Lord, though we ask that justice not be delayed any longer. The bowls are again full, as they were at the time of the first Exodus. Give Your people the grace to forgive, because You taught us to forgive as we also have been forgiven by You, and because You would not have a spirit of unforgiveness hinder the blessings You desire to pour out upon us. Let Your mercy fall, Lord, but never again let Your people fall asleep while the strong man enters and plunders the house of Your people. In Jesus' Name, amen.

My friend, look up. Look up, I urge you, and direct your gaze to all those souls reconciled to God who have crossed the Great River before us. They are in *Paradise*. The God of mercy did not fail them, and He is not going to fail us now. Christ be with you always. Amen.

---

* Psalm 30:5

PSALM 85

¹ *LORD, Thou hast been favourable unto Thy land:*
Thou hast brought back the captivity of Jacob.
² *Thou hast forgiven the iniquity of Thy people,*
Thou hast covered all their sin. Selah.
³ *Thou hast taken away all Thy wrath: Thou hast*
turned Thyself from the fierceness of Thine anger.
⁴ *Turn us, O God of our salvation,*
and cause Thine anger toward us to cease.
⁵ *Wilt Thou be angry with us for ever?*
wilt Thou draw out Thine anger to all generations?
⁶ *Wilt Thou not revive us again:*
that Thy people may rejoice in Thee?
⁷ *Shew us Thy mercy, O LORD,*
and grant us Thy salvation.
⁸ *I will hear what God the LORD will speak:*
for He will speak peace unto His people, and to His
saints: but let them not turn again to folly.
⁹ *Surely His salvation is nigh them that fear Him;*
that glory may dwell in our land.
¹⁰ *Mercy and truth are met together;*
righteousness and peace have kissed each other.
¹¹ *Truth shall spring out of the earth;*
and righteousness shall look down from heaven.
¹² *Yea, the LORD shall give that which is good;*
and our land shall yield her increase.
¹³ *Righteousness shall go before Him;*
and shall set us in the way of His steps.